MAKE THE Team.

BASKETBALL

BASKETBALL

A slammin' jammin' guide to super hoops!

Richard J. Brenner

A *Sports Illustrated For Kids* Book

First Edition

Library of Congress Cataloging-in-Publication Data

Brenner, Richard J., 1941–
    Make the team, basketball : a slammin' jammin' guide to super
hoops! / by Richard Brenner.—1st ed.
      p.   cm.
    "A Sports Illustrated for kids book."
    Summary: Instructions for improving basketball skills, discussing
dribbling, shooting, passing, defense, and offense, and how to handle
problems with coaches, parents, referees, and other players.
Includes a brief history of the sport.
    ISBN 0-316-10748-4 (hc)
    ISBN 0-316-10749-2 (pb)
    1. Basketball—Juvenile literature.   [1. Basketball.]   I. Title.
  GV885.1.B74 1990
  796.323'2—dc20

                                     89-48224
                                          CIP
                                            AC

Sports Illustrated For Kids Books is a joint imprint of Little, Brown and Company
and Warner Juvenile Books. This title is published in arrangement with
Cloverdale Press Inc.

10 9 8 7 6 5 4 3 2

BP

For further information regarding this title, write to
Little, Brown and Company, 34 Beacon Street, Boston, MA 02108.

Published simultaneously in Canada
by Little, Brown & Company (Canada) Limited

Printed in the United States of America

For Jason and Halle and our backyard games.
The ball bounced right for me when you two were born;
for Anita, for your invaluable help;
for Doug Berman, wherever you are,
thanks for being at the P.S. 238 night center,
for the basketball and the literature;
and for all the time and all the games,
and for all the boys at the Avenue P
(Col. David Marcus) Park and Sid's Candy Store.

CONTENTS

Chapter 1

FROM PEACH BASKETS TO MICHAEL JORDAN

Did you know that basketball is *the* great American sport? In the United States we like to think we invented basketball, baseball and football. But the roots of baseball and football can be traced to English sports— baseball developed from the game of cricket and football grew out of rugby and soccer. Only basketball is truly home-grown. It all began right here in this country nearly 100 years ago.

It was December 1891 and James Naismith, a physical education instructor at the Young Men's Christian Association (YMCA) Training School in Springfield, Massachusetts, wasn't happy. He and his students faced the dreary prospect of having to play indoors for the next several months. There wasn't much to choose from in the way of games. He wanted to think up something new.

One day the inventive teacher attached a peach basket to each end of the balcony in the school's gymnasium. Then he divided his class into two teams and told them to toss a soccer ball into the baskets. "Basketball" proved to be such a hit that when the winter season was over they moved the game outdoors. In the sport's earliest days sometimes as many as 100 people played in a single game!

Basketball's popularity got a big boost when someone realized that he could pick up the pace by cutting holes in the bottom of the baskets. Up until then janitors had been retrieving the balls by standing on stepladders! This innovation not only speeded up the game but also allowed the janitors to come down off their stepladders.

A few years later a sporting goods company produced the first ball designed specifically for basketball. It was much bouncier than a soccer ball and made dribbling a lot easier. In 1906 metal hoops were developed to replace the old peach baskets, and the first backboards were introduced.

The equipment and rules of the game have changed a lot over the years. Originally, for example, there were 9 players on a team because there had been 18 students in Naismith's class at the YMCA. Also, each basket scored counted as 3 points. And if a team committed three or more fouls the other team was awarded a point.

As basketball evolved its popularity grew quickly, particularly on the East Coast and in the Midwest! Before World War II, independent touring teams—-also called "barnstorming teams"—would play against each other in dance halls and barns where they would simply hang up backboards and baskets for the night.

After the war, two official leagues sprang up: the National Basketball League, which had the best players under contract, and the Basketball Association of America, which had agreements with most of the best arenas. By 1948 the NBL had gone out of business, and its best players and teams signed up with the BAA. In 1949 the League changed its name and the National Basketball Association was born. The new league had eight teams.

The big drawing card in the early days of the NBA was the Minneapolis Lakers with their star center, George Mikan. The Lakers won the League title in 1949 and in four of the next five seasons as well. At 6′ 10″, the broad-shouldered Mikan towered over most of his opponents. He was also a better athlete. That combination made him

James Naismith, the Massachusetts YMCA instructor who invented basketball.

a terror on the court. The Lakers surrounded Mikan with an all-star cast that included Slater Martin, one of the great playmakers of all time, and Jim Pollard, a sharp-shooting forward. The success of Mikan and the Lakers provided the new NBA with a foundation to grow on.

The League had a problem, though. Whenever a team built up a comfortable lead it would just pass the ball around and not shoot. By "stalling," the leading team could keep the opposition from getting the ball and catching up. Many of the games were very boring to watch. So in 1954 the NBA introduced the 24-second clock. With the clock came a new rule: When a team got possession of the ball, it would have to shoot within 24 seconds or else lose the ball to the other team. That changed everything! The pro game went from being slow and low-scoring to being fast and high-scoring. And with the new rule a team could come back and win even if it got behind by 20 or 30 points.

Three years after the Lakers' string of championships ended in 1954, another dominant center, 6′ 11″ Bill Russell led his team, the Boston Celtics, to an even longer run of championship seasons. Beginning with the 1956–1957 season the Celtics won an amazing 11 NBA titles in 13 years. Red Auerbach, the coach and later the president of the Celtics, always surrounded Russell with great players—Bob Cousy, John Havlicek and Sam and K. C. Jones were among Russell's outstanding teammates. But while other players came and went, Russell was the constant presence that connected all the Celtic teams.

Russell changed the way the game of basketball was played. Mikan had been a good athlete but he was a slow mover. Russell was quick and agile. Skills like Russell's had never been seen in someone so tall. His greatness did not come from his shooting and scoring but from his defensive skills and his rebounding. His ability to block shots and control rebounds allowed the Celtics to develop their fast break, in which they would move the ball from one end of the court to the other and score before the opposing team could catch up. The fast break became the most powerful weapon in the game and it became the Celtics' trademark. Not only did the fast break win games for Boston, it also made those games very exciting to watch. Fans began packing basketball arenas to see the action.

The NBA began expanding from its original eight teams and the league reached the West Coast when the Lakers moved to Los Angeles in 1960. New teams sprang up in many parts of the country. In 1967 a new league was formed, the American Basketball Association; although in 1976 the ABA went out of business, four of its teams—the Denver Nuggets, the Indiana Pacers, the New Jersey Nets and the San Antonio Spurs—joined the NBA.

Two other very important contributions came from the ABA: the three-point basket (shots made from more than 23' 9'' away are worth three points); and Julius Erving, the famous "Doctor J," one of basketball's brightest stars.

Earvin "Magic" Johnson and Larry Bird entered the NBA in 1979 and pro basketball became even more exciting. When Michael Jordan came along in 1984 the game took off like Michael himself on one of his amazing slam dunks! The NBA continued to expand, adding four more teams in the late 1980s.

Basketball has become a popular sport all over the

Cynthia Cooper of the U.S. Olympic basketball team in action at the 1988 Summer Games. The U.S. captured the gold medal with a 77–70 victory over the Yugoslavian national team.

world. Many good players from the United States are join-ing leagues in Europe, primarily in Spain and Italy. And some European stars such as Vlade Divac from Yugo-slavia and Alexander Volkov from the Soviet Union have joined NBA teams. Basketball is also an Olympic sport—the men started playing for medals in 1936 and the women started in 1976.

Basketball is also thriving on the high school and col-lege levels. The annual National Collegiate Athletic Asso-ciation (NCAA) tournament is considered to be *the* sports event of the year by many fans. Like players jumping for rebounds, the popularity of basketball continues to go up, up, UP!

About This Book

Make the Team: Basketball has been designed as a com-plete course in the game. Whether you're just getting started or have played a bit and want to improve, you'll find what you need in the pages to follow.

Before you turn to the actual "skills and drills" that make up the bulk of this book, be sure to read the over-view of the game that explains the rules, the players' roles and a variety of other basics. This will give you what you need to get started.

After you've been the skills and drills, the chapter called "putting it all together" explains the basic offensive and defensive strategies and tactics you'll need to know when game time arrives.

Throughout *Make the Team: Basketball* you'll find spe-cial boxes devoted to particular problems you may face while playing or learning to play basketball.

Finally, it's important to remember that, although you'll be reading this book as an *individual* who wants to play super hoops, basketball is a *team* sport. You'll never become as good a player as Magic Johnson or Larry Bird if you aren't a team player. That's the beauty of the game at any level—from pick-up games to the NBA finals.

Now let's talk basketball!

Chapter 2

EQUIPMENT

When it comes to playing basketball, you need just a few pieces of basic equipment—ball, sneakers and a water container. You might consider asking your parents to help pay for some of the gear, which will cost about $50.

If you think you and your parents might have trouble raising the money, talk to your coach or local youth league counselor to see if there are other options. Sometimes, for instance, local businessmen such as shops and banks sponsor teams and even buy them full uniforms. You may be able to find a used ball, and although you may prefer to play in the latest basketball shoes, you don't need the fanciest.

Balls

It's very helpful to have your own ball so you can practice by yourself in your yard or in a park when your friends aren't available. In addition, at team practices almost all the training exercises are done with a ball. If there aren't enough balls to go around the players have to stand around waiting for their turns, wasting valuable time.

There are two sizes of basketballs: the youth and women's size, which measures 28½ inches in circumference (all the way around the outside of the ball), and the regulation size, which measures 30 inches. Your coach will probably start you out with the smaller ball but you shouldn't feel embarrassed about this. All it means is that your hand isn't big enough yet for the regulation size. A good new basketball can cost anywhere from $13 to $30.

They can be bought at sporting-goods and department stores.

Sneakers

Once upon a time, buying a pair of sneakers was easy. Most basketball players wore low-cut sneakers made of canvas and rubber that came in either black or white. Today, basketball shoes come in an incredible variety of colors and styles and the selection can be confusing. The important points to consider are size, support, arch and traction.

Basketball is a game that requires constant running, jumping, twisting and pivoting. It's hard to do all these things if you're not wearing a well-made, properly fitted pair of shoes. Shoes that are too small will be uncomfortable, and shoes that are too large can make you trip and will certainly slow you down on the court.

Your sneakers should be firm but flexible and you should tie the laces securely enough to give your foot plenty of support. A good sneaker will also have a slight arch or cushion built into the bottom of it to support the arch on the bottom of your foot. You should also check with the salesperson to make sure that you are getting sneakers that have the proper soles (bottoms) for the surface you're going to be playing on. Certain patterns of bumps and ridges wear better and provide better traction on indoor floors and others are better for playing in the park or school yard.

As for the great high-top versus low-cut debate, high-tops seem to have won out. They offer much more ankle support which is crucial in a game with so many sideways moves and stops and starts. People who like low-cuts say that high-tops offer support but not flexibility. Try both styles and decide which you prefer.

Finally, as long as you take care of these basics, you can start to think about style (if you care) and the family budget. You can get all the sneaker you need for about $25–$30 and you can go all the way up to $200! It's up to your taste—and your wallet.

Here are some hints about sneaker shopping:

• A sporting-goods store will probably offer you a better selection of shoes than a regular shoe store. They will also have salespeople who are more knowledgeable about basketball.

• Shop toward the end of the day. Feet tend to swell a bit as the day goes on; sneakers that feel fine in the morning may feel uncomfortably tight in the afternoon.

• When you try on sneakers, wear the same type of socks you'll be wearing to play and practice.

• Don't be shy about running or practicing some basketball moves while you're in the store. (This doesn't mean you should bring your ball along!) Simply standing or walking in a new pair of sneakers won't give you a sense of how they will feel on the court. You may have to put up with some strange looks from other shoppers, however!

Socks

There's no big decision here. Whatever kind you're comfortable with is fine, whether cotton or nylon.

A Portable Drinking Container

This should be considered a piece of basic equipment. The plastic type with a built-in straw costs about $3. It's very important to take breaks regularly during practice and as often as you can during a game to drink some juice or water. While you're playing hard and perspiring your body is losing liquids; these liquids need to be replaced or you may get muscle cramps and heat exhaustion.

Chapter 3

The Warm-Up

Basketball players can only jump as high and run as far as their muscles will allow, so if you want to play your best you're going to have to keep in shape. You'll find that if you regularly practice the drills in this book you'll develop the stamina and leg strength you need to run the court and play at the top of your form for an entire game. A lot of games are decided in the closing minutes, and in the clutch it's the players who are in the best condition who give the best performances.

To reach your peak performance level a little sooner you can add a running program and some calisthenics, which are exercises like chinning and sit-ups, to your schedule. An effective running program for a basketball player should include distance running to build up leg strength and oxygen capacity. And wind sprints (short, top-speed runs) will simulate the demands you'll place on your body during a tough game. You might also spend some time practicing the boxer's shuffle—quick steps forward, back and to the sides as though you were in the ring with an opponent—to help your footwork and to build up the leg muscles you'll need for the quick sideways movements required on defense.

Getting in shape is important but doing it correctly without overdoing it is even more important. And it involves more than just exercise. It also involves eating sensibly and getting enough sleep.

You've probably heard the saying "You are what you eat." Stop and think about that for a minute. If you fill your body with a lot of junk food, what does that make *you*? An automobile won't run well on cheap fuel and if you stuff your face with potato chips and chocolate, you're not going to function very well either. Make sure you eat a balanced diet from the four basic food groups: dairy, meat, grains, and fruits and vegetables. Don't eat too much food that is high in calories and low in nutrition.

Warming Up

Warming up for a few minutes before a practice or game is good preparation for both your mind and your body. Warming up sends your brain a wake-up signal and gets your body ready for more strenuous exercise. It's also a good way to avoid pulling a muscle, which can happen easily if you exert yourself suddenly.

A good way to start your warm-up is with a series of stretching exercises.

● To stretch the *hamstring* muscle, which is the long muscle that runs from the back of your knee to the buttocks:

1. Holding on to a bench, a fence or a friend, lift one foot off the ground and bend your leg at the knee.

2. Grab your foot and hold it against your backside for a count of 10.

3. Repeat three times with each leg.

Eventually you'll be able to do this without holding on to anything.

● To stretch the *groin* muscle, which is the muscle in the fold between the lower part of your body and your upper thigh:

1. Sit on the floor or ground.

2. Put the soles of your feet together, with your knees

27

as close as possible to the ground and pointed outward.

3. Grasp your ankles and hold that position for a count of 10.

4. Relax and repeat three times.

● To stretch your *calf* muscles:

1. Get in a push-up position, but put one knee on the ground.

2. Put your weight on the toes of your other foot and then push the heel down until you feel a slight pull.

3. Hold that position for a count of 10.

4. Relax and repeat three times with each leg.

● To stretch your *back* muscles:

1. Lying on your back, raise one leg, and grabbing the leg right below the knee, slowly bring it up to your chest.

2. Keeping your other leg straight and your head on the ground, hold this position for a count of 10.

3. Repeat three times with each leg.

● To stretch your *shoulder:*

1. Move one arm across your body, almost as if you were going to take a backhand swing.

2. Grasp the elbow of the arm in motion with your other hand and gently pull the arm further across your body.

3. Hold for a count of 10 and repeat three times with each arm.

Now that you are stretched, you should do a general warm-up such as jogging lightly or running in place for a few minutes. Remember, you're not trying to break any speed records and you don't want to use up your energy before you take the court.

After you've completed the general warm-up, you should work on the techniques that you will use during a game. In the following chapters you'll find drills that will help you do this.

There might be some people on your team who don't understand the value of warm-ups and think they're a waste of time. If you have any doubts about the importance of warming up and stretching, just ask yourself why all professional teams insist that their players warm up before they play or practice. This is how champions are made and kept healthy!

Finally: *Don't begin any exercise program without first consulting your parents or guardian and someone, such as a gym teacher, who is knowledgeable about training programs. This will guarantee that you come up with the program that's best for you.*

Chapter 4

A Bird's-Eye View

Before we start talking about the actual skills you'll need to develop in order to play basketball, let's take a look at the game as a whole. It's important to understand how all the various parts work together. We'll begin with . . .

The Court

The outer dimensions of a basketball court, as well as some of the interior measurements, vary depending on the age level of the players. Professional and college courts are usually 94 feet long and 50 feet wide; high school courts are slightly shorter, about 84 feet; and leagues for younger players often use courts that are both shorter and narrower than high school courts. The size of a basketball court also depends on the size of your school's gym, your local park or even your driveway, if you're lucky enough to be able to play hoops at home! But no matter what size they are, all basketball courts have certain features in common:

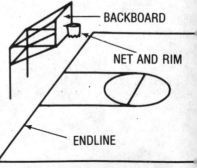

The layout of a baketball court

BACKBOARD

NET AND RIM

ENDLINE

The court is a rectangle. The long lines of the rectangle are called *sidelines*. The short ends of the rectangle are called *end lines*. The *midcourt line* (parallel to the end lines) divides the court in half across the middle. In the exact middle of the court is a *center circle* which is 4 feet in diameter. Surrounding the center circle is the *restraining circle* or *ring*, which is 12 feet in diameter.

There are *backboards* at either end of the court. Although it sounds as though they should be made of wood, most of them are fiberglass these days. (Other materials are sometimes used.) Backboards may be either rectangular or fan-shaped and are placed parallel to and 4 feet in from the end lines. The *rim* is attached to the center of the backboard exactly 10 feet off the floor and a *net* is attached to the rim.

At each end of the court two lines extend 19 feet out into the court to the *free throw line* or *foul line*. The rectangular area formed by these lines is called the *key* or the *free throw lane* or just the *lane*, and it is 12 feet wide.

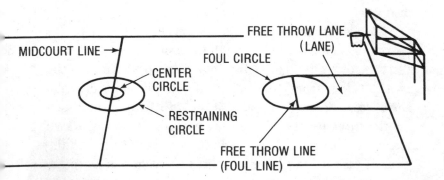

MIDCOURT LINE →
FREE THROW LANE
(LANE)
FOUL CIRCLE
CENTER CIRCLE
RESTRAINING CIRCLE
FREE THROW LINE
(FOUL LINE)

From the free throw line, players take shots at the basket after they have been fouled; this is discussed later in this chapter. The free throw line forms the center line of the *foul circle*, also to be explained later.

Length of Game

The National Basketball Association (NBA) divides its games into four 12-minute quarters. Colleges use two 20-minute halves, high schools use four 8-minute quarters and younger teams usually play four 6-minute quarters.

If two teams are tied at the end of the final period, overtime periods are played—five minutes each in the NBA and in college, three minutes each in high school games—until someone wins. There is generally a 10-minute rest period between halves; rest periods between quarters usually last only 2 or 3 minutes.

Scoring

There are two ways to score points: field goals and free throws.

Field goals are shots from the court. When a player shoots or taps the ball through the opposing team's basket, he scores a field goal. It is worth two points unless the shot is taken from beyond an arc known as the *three-point line*, in which case it is worth—you guessed right!—three points. The three-point line is an arc drawn at varying distances from each basket, depending on the level of play. In the NBA the three-point line is 23 feet 9 inches from the basket. In college and high-school hoops the three-point line is 19 feet 9 inches from the basket.

Kareem Abdul Jabbar of the Los Angeles Lakers was one of the greatest centers ever. His 38,387 regular-season points and 5,762 playoff points are both NBA records.

Free throws or *foul shots* are shots from the foul line. When personal fouls occur players are sometimes allowed to take free throws. (Fouls are discussed later in this chapter.) A successful free throw or foul throw is worth one point.

The Line-Up

Each team puts five players on the court: a center, two forwards and two guards. The center and the two forwards are known as the *front court* or the *front line* because they play up front near the basket. They are usually the tallest players on the team and their main responsibilities are to score and rebound.

The *center* is generally the team's tallest player and its best rebounder and shot-blocker. And the best centers are always good passers. The center usually plays close to the basket (but outside the lane) in what is called a *low post*. When the center comes out to play past the foul line he is said to be playing *high post*.

If you watch a lot of pro or college basketball you'll hear some other terms. As players become more skilled, their coaches can use those skills for specific purposes. For instance pro and college coaches often team a *power forward* with a *small forward*. The power forward is usually a few inches taller than the small forward and tends to be a better rebounder and inside scorer (in other words, scoring from close to the basket). The small forward is usually quicker and a better ball handler and outside shooter than the power forward.

Similarly, many pro and college teams pair a *point*

36

Two of the best forwards in basketball history—Larry Bird of the Boston Celtics and Julius (Dr. J) Erving of the Philadelphia 76ers.

Kim Mulkey of the U.S. Olympic basketball team doing what guards do best—dribbling the ball upcourt.

guard with an *off guard*. The point guard acts as the team's quarterback, directing the attack and making most of the passes. The off guard is also known as the *shooting guard* and as you can guess from that name, is usually a good outside shooter and high scorer. The two guards together make up a team's *backcourt*.

Referees

There are usually two officials assigned to youth league games. They run up and down the court following the action, and have complete authority in calling violations and fouls and in making other calls, such as whether the ball has gone out of bounds.

Fouls

There are two groups of fouls: *personal fouls* and *technical fouls*. Personal fouls occur when there is illegal body contact between opposing players. Here are some of the more common personal fouls:

- charging—when an offensive player runs into a defensive player who is standing still
- blocking—when an offensive player obstructs a defensive player, or when a defensive player obstructs an offensive player
- hacking—when a defensive player hits an offensive player with the hand or arm
- holding—when a defensive player holds onto an offensive player in order to slow him down or alter a shot
- loose ball—when a foul is committed but neither team has possession of the ball, for example during a scramble for a rebound

If the referee rules that a defensive player committed an *intentional* foul or that the foul occurred while the offensive player was in the act of shooting, then the fouled player is given two free throws. In other cases, the number of foul shots awarded depends on the game situation and the rules of the particular league.

Each player is allowed a certain number of personal fouls, usually five. If that limit is exceeded the player has *fouled out* of the game and cannot return.

In most leagues there is also a limit on how many personal fouls a team may commit in a period. Once a team goes over the limit the opposing team gets an extra free throw each time it gets fouled. For example, a two-shot foul would turn into a three-chances-to-make-two situation, or a one-shot foul would turn into a one-and-one situation in which the player taking the free throw gets to take a second if he makes the first.

Technical fouls are called when a player or coach argues with a referee or uses abusive language. A technical foul is also called if a player or coach breaks a rule, such as calling a timeout after the team has used up all its timeouts.

When a technical foul is called against a team the other team is awarded a free throw. The coach of the other team may select any one of the five players on the floor at the time of the foul to shoot the free throw. The team taking the foul shot retains possession of the ball.

If a player or coach commits two technical fouls in the same game he is ejected from the game. Anyone who hits a player or official on purpose is ejected and will probably be suspended for some future games as well.

? ■ **WHAT IF** somebody on the other team is playing dirty?

If somebody is playing dirty and the referee isn't catching the action, it can really make you mad. The only thing to do is stay calm—*never* retaliate. Referees may miss the initial foul, but they almost always nab the "payback." Wait for a play to stop and then let the referees know, in a polite way, that you're being mugged and you'd appreciate it if they would keep an eye on the culprit.

Violations

A *violation* has occurred when the rules of basketball are broken. In most cases, a violation is less serious than a foul. Unless a foul has also been committed the penalty for a violation is usually loss of possession of the ball. Violations are also called *turnovers*. The most common violations that result in loss of the ball are the following:

1. Failure to put the ball into play from out of bounds within 5 seconds.

2. Failure to move the ball from the backcourt to the frontcourt within ten seconds.

3. When an offensive player remains in the lane for more than three seconds without being in the act of shooting.

4. When an offensive player deliberately kicks or punches the ball.

5. When a player with the ball takes more than one

step without dribbling. This is called walking, steps *or* traveling.

6. When a player who has stopped dribbling starts again without either giving up or temporarily losing possession of the ball. This is called a double dribble.

7. When a team fails to take a shot within 24 seconds of gaining possession of the ball. (In college a shot must be taken within 45 seconds.)

Some violations do not result in loss of possession but carry other penalties. Here are two examples:

1. When a player taking a free throw steps on or over the free throw line while taking the shot, the basket, if good, doesn't count.

2. No player is allowed to step into the foul lane while a free throw is being taken until the ball has touched either the rim or the backboard. If a defensive player breaks this rule and the free throw is missed the shooter gets another chance. If the free throw is made, however, the shot stands. If an offensive player breaks this rule and the free throw is made the shot doesn't count. If the shot is missed, the defensive team takes possession of the ball unless it was the first shot of a two-shot foul.

Starts and Restarts

Every basketball game starts with a *tip-off* at midcourt in the center circle. The two centers—or if not the center, a team's best jumper—jump for a ball that a referee throws into the air between them. They try to tip the ball to one of their teammates--all players except those involved in the tip-off must stay outside the restraining circle—and the action begins.

Basketball is played in a continuous flow until a period ends unless:

1. A foul occurs. If a shooting foul is called, foul shots are awarded to the team that was fouled; if a non-shooting foul occurs, the team that was fouled puts the ball into play.

2. The ball is knocked out of bounds. The team that last touched the ball before it went out of bounds loses possession of the ball. The other team has five seconds to get the ball back into play. If it takes longer than that, the ball goes back to the first team.

3. Two opposing players hold onto the ball at the same time. An example is when two players are fighting for a rebound and the referee rules that they both have gained possession of the ball. In some leagues the two players would take a *jump ball* either at the foul circle or at center court, whichever is closer to the spot where the play ended. A jump ball is the same thing as the tip-off with the referee throwing the ball up in the middle. In other leagues teams alternate taking possession and keep track of the turns with a *possession arrow*. The team that loses the tip-off at the opening of the game gains possession on the first play in which the possession arrow is called into use.

Practicing

In this book we'll show you how to dribble a basketball with either hand, make pinpoint passes and shoot accurate jump shots. You'll find out how to set picks and run plays like the give-and-go and the pick-and-roll. But the

43

only way to learn those skills is to *practice*.

Practicing can be fun but it can also get pretty boring sometimes, especially when you do the same drill over and over. Try to remember that repeating the drills is the best way to learn new skills. It's like playing the piano—you can't make music if you haven't practiced the scales.

You might get frustrated at times because it's taking you a long time to learn something. You might even begin to get discouraged and think, "I'm never going to learn how to do this." But if you stick to it and really work at it you *will* learn how to do it. Remember, millions of kids all over the country have practiced the same drills and felt the same frustration. They went on to play and enjoy basketball. So will you!

Teamwork

Teamwork is the basic foundation of successful basketball. It's the magic that turns a disorganized bunch of kids into a functioning group. Sure, you need the skills to play the game, but you have to blend those skills with the skills of the other players in order to have a team. Even a group of all-stars wouldn't win very often if they didn't play together as a team. Just imagine a stage full of talented musicians who are each playing a different tune and ignoring the conductor. They might be great musicians but they will never become a great orchestra until they begin to play together.

The essential principle of teamwork is that players must always put the good of the team ahead of any dreams of personal glory. Everyone would like to score the basket that wins the game. But when a player finds himself in a position to take a pretty good jump shot and then sees a teammate completely unguarded near the basket, as a team player he will pass the ball. And the player who scores the basket, even while he's jumping up and down in celebration, should always remember that it took a lot of work by the team to set up that shot.

Teamwork isn't just passing the ball and helping out on defense. It also means having a good attitude toward your teammates and coach. It's about cheering a teammate for making a good play or learning a new skill and about offering encouragement instead of blame when a teammate makes a mistake. Teamwork means working on your own skills so you can contribute to the overall success of the team. Showing up on time for practices and games is a sign of teamwork: It shows cooperation and caring, two basics of good teamwork.

Your Coach

Coaches are the men and women who must take the players—you and your teammates—and try to create a winning squad. They have to figure out who works best at each position, help everyone improve their skills at each position, and then show the individual players how to function as a team. They have to try to get along with their players and discipline them when things go wrong. And they have to keep up a team's spirits after losses because even good teams don't always win. What a job!

Coaches come in all ages, shapes and sizes, and they have different levels of ability, just like players. Your coach may know a lot or only a little about basketball and how to teach skills or coach a team. Coaches also have different personalities—some are more friendly and understanding than others.

Chances are that your coach likes kids and sports. As long as your coach is fair and not abusive, remember that he's giving a lot of time to the team and doing the best job of coaching that he knows how to do.

One way you can show respect for your coach is to show up on time for all games and practices. If you can't make a game or a practice, let the coach know as far in advance as possible. Another way to show respect is to listen when your coach talks and to save the horsing around for after practice.

Sometimes a coach and a player have different ideas about which position a player is best suited for. It's helpful to remember that from the coach's point of view (and yours, too, ideally), all the positions on a basketball team are equally important. They work like the pieces of a jigsaw puzzle. Each piece is just as important as the next, and if they don't fit together you don't get the complete picture.

It's all right to ask the coach to let you try a new position, but choose the right moment. Don't bring it up during a game or in the middle of practice when a coach has other things on his mind. After all, you wouldn't like it if a teammate started talking about next week's game in the middle of this week's practice, would you? Part of being on a team means you have to accept the coach's decision without kicking up a fuss even though you may not agree with it. Arguing will only make it harder for you, your coach and your teammates to work together.

Also try to understand that the coach may not always

? *HOW DO* I tell my parents I don't want them around when I'm playing, or how do I tell them I wish they'd come and watch for a change?

Some parents act as if they're the chief cheerleader, coaching expert and head referee all rolled into one. If your parents get a little carried away during a game and it bothers, you politely explain your feelings to them. Other parents act in exactly the opposite way—they just aren't interested in watching a bunch of kids try to put a ball through a hoop. If that bothers you, let them know you would appreciate their support. But keep in mind that *you* signed up to play ball, not your parents. You probably don't get all excited about your dad's golf game or your mom's aerobics class. If basketball doesn't turn them on, don't get upset. Just play ball and have a good time.

be able to give you the attention you need or want. There are ten players on a team, with five starting positions, and only one coach. Remember, the coach is also a part of the team and deserves your cooperation.

Playing for Fun

The most important reason to play basketball is that you enjoy the game. You shouldn't play basketball because someone else wants you to, and you shouldn't play basketball if you prefer individual sports. But if you like running, shooting and working together with other players on a team and if you're willing to practice, then basketball is the game for you!

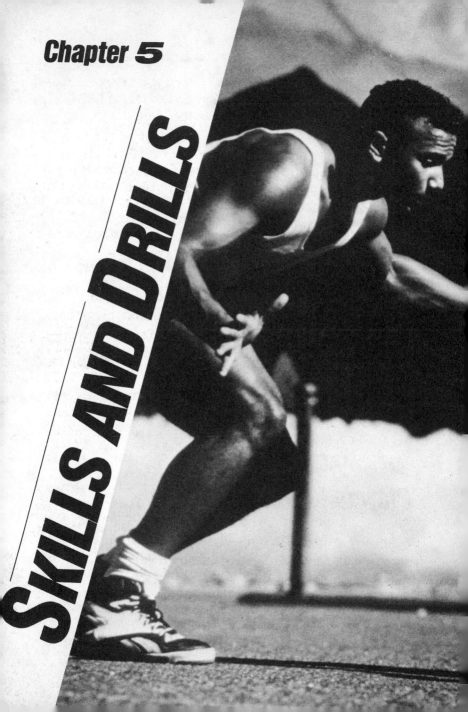

Chapter 5

SKILLS AND DRILLS

*I*n earlier chapters we've mentioned many skills. Here's where we explain them so you can learn how to master them. They are all necessary if you want to become a complete basketball player, but you don't have to learn them all at once. You should work at your own pace and in a way that makes you feel comfortable.

Before you practice a new technique, remember the old saying, "Don't try to run before you can walk." Learning how to perfect a new skill takes time and it's important that you learn to perform the skill correctly. Shortcuts won't help. You may be a gifted athlete but no one is born knowing how to shoot a ball properly or how to dribble with either hand. To do it well takes determination, dedicated practice and patience. Too many people are willing to settle for being mediocre. Take your time and get it right.

The Basic Offensive Stance

No matter what position you play, you need to learn the basic offensive stance. It's also called the *ready* stance because it gets you ready to do everything you have to do on offense. When you're in the ready position you're all set to receive a pass, or if you already have the ball, to dribble, pass or shoot.

Get into the ready stance as follows:

1. Stand with your feet shoulder-width apart, one foot slightly in front of the other. Your knees should be bent slightly.

2. Hold your arms in front of you at chest level, with your elbows bent and tucked in close to your body and

50

*The basic
offensive stance*

your palms facing out. Your head should be up and you should be alert.

Basketball is a very fast game with lots of sudden stops and starts. In the ready position you'll always be able to handle the speed and the ball.

The Pivot

A pivot is defined as that on which something turns. In basketball the "pivot" is the ball of your foot. It is also the name of the basic movement in basketball. When you have the ball you'll use the pivot to maneuver for a shot or to make a pass when you're being guarded. When you're moving without the ball you'll use the pivot to spin or shift your position to try to get open to receive a pass.

Here's how to pivot:

1. Raise the heel of one foot.

2. Turn on the ball of that foot in the direction you want to go. Your other foot is called your free *foot—you can move it as much as you want to.*

Remember, you can't change your pivot foot while you're holding the ball. You can pivot on one foot or the other as much as you want as long as you don't lift your toes off the ground and you can move your free foot any way you want to. But once you establish which foot you're using as your pivot foot on a particular play, you can't then change your mind and pivot on the other foot. If you do you'll be called for taking too many steps, also known as walking, and that means turning the ball over to the other team.

Shooting

Putting the ball in the basket is the ultimate aim of a basketball player. Everything a team does on offense is a means to that end. There are many different types of shots, but two elements are common to all shots that are made correctly. The first is that the power for the shot comes from the feet and flows up from your toes through your ankles, up through your flexed knees, hips, upper body, arms, wrist, hand and finally the fingertips. All this should happen in one continuous, fluid motion.

The second element in shooting a basketball is the position of your arm. Your upper arm should form a right angle with your forearm (like a capital letter "L"). Your wrist should be bent back so that your hand is almost at a 90-degree angle to your forearm and parallel to your upper arm. Your fingers should grip the ball from behind

The perfect shot. Notice that this player's upper arm and forearm form a right angle.

and slightly below the ball's center point. Every part of your arm should be lined up with the basket. After all, you are aiming at a target. Make sure that your elbow doesn't slide out sideways or you'll alter the angle of your delivery and the accuracy of your shot.

When you shoot the ball extend your arm up toward the basket, flick your wrist up and forward and let the ball roll off your fingertips. This will give your shots backspin and the soft touch that all good shooters have.

The descriptions of all the basic shots that you're about to read may sound complicated at first. But if you work on the movements in front of a mirror they'll all come together. When you start shooting don't be too worried about sinking your shots. Concentrate instead on your technique and the rhythm of your motion. Try to become

The basic steps for shooting a basketball

aware of how your body feels when you've achieved that rhythm and then try to duplicate it on every shot you take. If your form is fluid and you practice regularly, accuracy will follow. Practice shooting from different spots around the basket so you learn to shoot comfortably from all angles.

Some coaches suggest that you try to put the ball in the basket just over the front rim. Others teach players to imagine a little hole in the center of the rim and to aim for that. Experiment with both techniques to find out which one works best for you.

The Layup

The *layup* is the easiest and most basic shot. It is made from near the basket either off the dribble or from a pass.

(*Dribbling* is moving the ball around the court with a series of controlled bounces. We'll discuss the technique in detail later in this chapter.) The ball is banked off the backboard into the basket. Which part of the backboard you aim for will depend on the angle from which you approach the basket. But in most cases your spot will be within the square painted on the backboard right above the basket.

To take the shot with your right hand, start off about 10 feet away from the basket, angled off to the right. Dribble toward the basket, timing your release so that you end up taking your last step with your left foot. As you take that last step hold the ball with two hands. The left hand should be in front of the ball and the right hand in back and toward the bottom. Then jump off your left foot, keeping your eyes on the spot on the backboard that you want the ball to hit. Take your left hand away from the ball, extend your right arm fully and release the ball at the top of your jump with a soft forward flick of your right wrist.

To take the shot with your left hand, reverse the steps outlined above. In the beginning you should only shoot with your stronger hand and concentrate on achieving a smooth technique. As soon as you get comfortable with your strong hand, work on developing a layup with your other hand. Being able to shoot with either hand will make you more difficult to defend against.

If you have trouble coordinating the dribble, the jump and the shot, forget about the dribble and the jump for now. Stand a step away from the basket off to the right side (if you're shooting right-handed). Take one step with your left foot, go up on your toes, take the ball up, raise

The layup

David Robinson of the San Antonio Spurs dribbling close to the basket, trying to work his way in for an easy layup.

your right foot, and lay the ball in. When you get the knack of shooting like this, gradually work in the dribble and the jump.

The Reverse Layup

The *reverse layup* is used when you dribble the ball under the basket from one side to the other and then put the shot up. When you execute this move properly the basket acts as a screen between you and your defender. If you're going to shoot the ball with your right hand, cross over from the left side to the right. Time your dribble so that your last step will put you in a position to pivot on your left foot and shoot the layup. As you take that last step, start to bring the ball up with both hands. Your left hand should be in front and under the ball and your right hand behind the ball and slightly under its center point. You should also begin to turn your shoulders square to the backboard. Then pivot toward the basket on the ball of your left foot as you flex your right knee, take the ball in your right hand and fully extend your right arm. Jump off the left foot and put the ball off the backboard with a soft flick of your wrist. To take the shot with your left hand, reverse the procedure.

The One-hand Set Shot

The *one-hand set shot* is the basic outside shot for most young players. Start by holding the ball in both hands at about the level of your eyes and slightly off center toward your shooting side. (If you hold the ball dead center in front of your face, it will block your view of the basket.) Place your shooting foot slightly in front of your other foot. Flex your knees, bring the ball up and bend your wrist back so that your arm is in the proper position. Then in one smooth motion rise up on the balls of your feet, straighten your legs, extend your arms fully and release the ball with your fingertips. You trigger the release by flexing your elbow and flipping your wrist forward and then down for the follow-through. Remember to start with the wrist flexed all the way back and to shoot the ball *up* as well as forward.

The jump shot

The Jump Shot

The *jump shot* is the most effective and widely used outside shot in basketball because it is so difficult to block, but young players sometimes have trouble with it. It's impossible to make the jump shot until the muscles in your legs, arms, shoulders and back are well developed. If you find that your body isn't ready, just be patient. You can't rush Mother Nature. A lack of muscular development will also limit the range from which you can make the jump shot so don't get over-anxious and try to force awkward shots from too far away. If you do, you'll wind up with poor technique and hurt your chances of developing into a good shooter.

To take a jump shot, hold the ball with two hands. Your non-shooting hand should be placed either in front of the ball or on the side, whichever feels more comfortable. Your shooting hand should be behind the ball. Bend your knees slightly, move the ball from chest level to just above your eyes, and spring off the balls of your feet. As you go up, cock your elbow and wrist back to the proper shooting position. When you reach the top of your jump, release the ball by flexing your elbow and following through with a forward and downward flick of the wrist. Keep your elbow tight to your body and your eyes on the basket.

Some players shoot from just above their eyes while others fully extend their arms. Extending your arms will make the shot more difficult to block, but you should find the position that works best for you. From certain angles a lot of players prefer to use the backboard to bank the jump shot rather than shooting straight at the basket. Experiment and see which way gives you the best results.

Akeem Olajuwon of the Houston Rockets pulls up for a jump shot, beating his defender (left). Two points for Akeem!

The Foul Shot

When making a *foul shot* from the free throw line, use the shooting technique you feel most comfortable with. Most players use the one-hand set shot but younger players often use the two-hand underhand technique because it's easier for them to generate the power they need for the ball to reach the basket. Rick Barry, one of the best free throw shooters in the history of the NBA, used the underhand shot.

Whatever method you select, you should always try to relax by following a set routine. Some players take deep breaths; others wiggle their hands to get loose or stare at the basket, focusing on a specific spot. Most players also bounce the ball a certain number of times before each shot. Establishing a routine will help you to concentrate on the shot.

To shoot the underhand foul shot, stand with your feet just behind the free throw line, shoulder-width apart. Place your hands on the sides of the ball, thumbs pointed forward, just below the center of the ball which is held at chest level. Begin by bending your knees and bending forward. Lower the ball so that it is between your knees. Your fingers should now be pointed downward and the backs of your hands should be almost touching the insides of your knees. Straighten your knees, rise up on your toes and bring the ball forward and upward. On the way up, fully extend your arms. When your hands are about at chest level release the ball with a backward flip of your wrists. Complete your follow through by raising your hands above your head with your fingers pointed skyward.

Shooting Drills

When you practice shooting, concentrate on your form. Make sure you have each technique down pat. Don't try to rush your shots. Being able to shoot quickly is important because that's what you have to do in a game, but first you have to develop form. Speed comes later. And don't shoot from "beyond your range," that is, farther from the basket than you feel comfortable.

The first shot to practice is the layup. Start out to the right of the key and drive in for the shot. Repeat 10 times, then switch to the left side of the key and put the ball up with your left hand. It will probably feel strange shooting with your left hand (or your right if you're a lefty) at first. But stick with it because the ability to shoot accurately with either hand will make you a much better player. Next try 10 crossover layups with each hand. Then find a free throw style that's comfortable for you and shoot 20 foul shots.

To practice your outside shots, pick five spots around

? WHAT IF I get hurt?

If you get hurt during a game, *don't* try to play through the pain. Stop playing and let the referee know you are injured. If you go down during a game or practice and feel pain or dizziness *don't* try to get up. Stay down and wait for your coach or the referee to check you out. And if you do suffer an injury, follow the doctor's instructions and give yourself enough time to heal.

the basket and within your shooting range. One way to do this is to play "Around the World"—take one shot from near the end line then one from halfway between the end line and the key, then from straight on, then from the other side of the key, and finally from near the end line opposite where you began. This will help you get used to shooting from different angles. Start with a one-hand set shot. Take a shot from each of the five spots then shoot your way back to the first spot. Repeat for the jump shots. You're probably not going to have the same range on every shot so don't forget to adjust the distance and concentrate on your form and accuracy.

If you're practicing with a friend you can alternate being the shooter and rebounder. Whoever is doing the rebounding should go up as if it's a real game and practice throwing outlet passes by throwing the ball back to the shooter as if the shooter is a teammate breaking upcourt.

After you've spent a lot of time working on your form and improving your accuracy, start increasing your speed. You can do this by taking the outlet pass and going straight up for the shot. On days when you have to practice alone, toss the ball up in the air, grab it and shoot. If you find your technique or accuracy falling off, slow down until you're in control again.

Another game you can play to practice your shooting is called "Beat the Ghost." Either you earn a point or the "ghost" does. You start at the free throw line. If you make the free throw you get a point and can take five shots from five spots around the basket. But every time you miss a shot, including the free throw, the "ghost" gets a point. Play to 20 points.

Rebounding

Strong rebounding is essential for a winning team. In most games more than half the shots taken are going to be missed. The team that gathers in those missed shots—in other words, the team that "controls the boards"—usually wins the game.

Being tall and a good jumper are definite pluses for becoming a good rebounder but strong desire and a determined attitude are just as important. Even in the NBA, the land of giants, most rebounds are snared below the level of the rim so you don't have to be seven feet tall or have pogo sticks for legs. Charles Oakley of the New York Knicks and Charles Barkley of the Philadelphia 76ers aren't all that tall and they aren't going to win any high jumping contests. But each season they are among the league leaders in rebounds because once the ball is in the air they own it.

The techniques for grabbing *defensive rebounds* (rebounds that come off your opponents' basket or backboard) are similar to those used for snatching *offensive rebounds* (rebounds that come off the basket you're shooting at). The major difference is that when you are on defense you should always try to be in good rebounding position, which means having your body between the basket and your opponent. When you are on offense you will most likely have to maneuver into that position, since you've been concentrating on being in good shooting position. Here are the keys that will unlock the secrets of successful rebounding:

1. Move *toward the basket as soon as a shot is taken*

with the attitude that the ball belongs to you.

2. *Get* good position *by anticipating where the ball will bounce off the rim or backboard and getting there quickly. (A little hint: Roughly 80 percent of shots missed from one side of the basket get rebounded on the other side.)*

3. Box out *your opponent by putting your body between him and the basket. Once you have that position, extend your arms, slightly bent at the elbows, so the player won't be able to go around you.*

4. Balance *your body by keeping your feet shoulder-width apart and your knees slightly bent. Get up on the balls of your feet, ready to spring.*

5. Time *your jump so you catch the ball when you're*

The correct way to box out an opponent and get into position for a rebound

at your highest point. Keep your arms fully extended and your fingers widely spread. Be ready to jump again if someone has tipped the ball back toward the basket and missed. (Tip-in baskets happen when an offensive player gets enough of his hands or fingers on the ball to send it into the basket before it has been rebounded.)

6. After you grab the ball, protect it. Sometimes this means bringing the ball close to your body and sometimes it means holding the ball above your head. It all depends on the situation on the floor, including the height of the players around you.

7. Be alert and know what you want to do with the ball. If you pull down a defensive rebound you'll want to make an outlet pass or start to dribble. If you pull down an offensive "board" (another word for rebound), you'll probably want to go right back up for a shot. If you're covered, pass the ball out to an open teammate.

8. If you can't grab the ball, try to keep it alive by tapping it. And then go right up after it again.

Remember, good rebounding depends on desire, determination and good positioning.

Rebounding Drills

Rebounding drills are easy to do on your own. It's almost like shooting baskets by yourself except for one thing: You're going to try and miss on purpose so that there will be rebounds for you to practice with!

To warm up for a rebounding drill, station yourself below the backboard. With your arms above your head jump as high as you can 10 times. Take a breath and then start lobbing balls high against the backboard so that they bounce off. Go up as high as you can and grab the ball. The first 10 times you grab it, pivot to your left to throw an imaginary outlet pass. The next 10 times, pivot to your right.

Before you go up for the rebound, pretend you're boxing out an opponent. Spread your arms and flex your knees before you jump up with your arms high above your head. When you come down with the ball, imagine that you're surrounded by opponents and that you have to protect it from grasping hands. Take 10 more practice boards but instead of throwing outlet passes, go right up with a shot. Shoot 5 times with your left hand and 5 times with your right hand.

Dribbling

Every player should learn how to become a skilled dribbler—with *either* hand. Being a good dribbler will add an important dimension to your game and make you a greater asset to your team. Dribbling allows you to:

1. Move the ball up the court quickly when you can't pass it to a teammate.

2. Keep control of the ball while a teammate moves into position to receive a pass or while you move to a better spot from which to make a pass.

3. Drive to the basket on your own.

As fundamental as dribbling is, it's just as important that it not be overdone. Unnecessary dribbling destroys the concept of teamwork because four players end up standing around watching one player. It is also a slower

This team's frontcourt should have no trouble grabbing the rebound. They have boxed out the opposing players,

their eyes are squarely on the ball and, most important, they look like they want the ball.

way of moving the ball than passing or shooting. So learn to dribble well but also learn *when* to dribble.

Always dribble with your fingertips, never your palms. You can control the ball better that way and keep it from bouncing too high—try to keep it at waist level. Your arm from your elbow to your fingers should act as a pump to

The basic dribbling stance. Remember to dribble with your fingertips and to watch the court, not the ball.

push the ball down. You shouldn't slap at the ball or tap it. Keep your wrist relaxed.

Begin to practice by dribbling in place. As soon as you feel comfortable doing that, start to walk around while you're dribbling. Concentrate on using the proper technique and don't worry about how fast you're going. After you've mastered the walking dribble, pick up your pace to a jog and gradually move to the full-speed dribble. Remember, you're not in a race. You're trying to master a

Isiah Thomas of the Detroit Pistons, guarded by Michael Cooper of the Los Angeles Lakers, dribbles while looking for a passing or shooting opportunity.

skill at a pace that's comfortable for you.

Always keep your head up and your eyes on the court rather than on the ball. As Red Auerbach, the former coach of the Boston Celtics, used to say, "The floor is flat and the ball is round, so you don't have to look for it." If you watch the ball instead of where you're going a defender is likely to steal the ball away from you. Also, if your eyes are on the ball you'll never see if a teammate is open for a pass or if you're in position to take a shot.

At first you'll definitely feel more comfortable dribbling with your strong hand—that is, the one you use to write or throw with. That's O.K. But if you want to be a complete player you'll have to be able to dribble with either hand. So make sure you pay special attention to developing your weaker hand.

There are many different dribbling techniques you can use, depending on the circumstances. When there are many players crowding your area of the court or when you're looking to set up a play or make a pass, use the *con-*

The control dribble

trol dribble, bouncing the ball between waist- and knee-high. Bend your knees slightly and hunch your shoulders forward while keeping your back fairly straight. Dribbling in a crouch allows you to control the ball better and to move more quickly.

Keep your non-dribbling arm bent at the elbow and away from your body to help you balance and to help shield the ball from defenders. But keep the arm relaxed, not stiff, and don't use it as a battering ram. It's there to protect the ball, not to attack a defender.

The speed dribble

The Speed Dribble

When you're racing down the court, use the *speed dribble*. With the speed dribble you push the ball out in front of you a bit more and you don't move in a crouched position. Lean your body forward and let the ball bounce higher, between waist- and chest-high. Keep your shoulders square to the direction you're moving and keep your non-dribbling arm out, your body relaxed and your eyes up the court.

The Change-of-pace Dribble

The *change-of-pace dribble* involves suddenly changing the speed at which you are moving and the height at which you're dribbling the ball. A sudden spurt of speed and lowering the height of the dribble will often allow you to move past or go around the player guarding you or make him commit a foul. See what happens, for example, when you approach a player at a trot using the control dribble and then suddenly rush past him by picking up your pace and lowering the dribble to knee level. You need to master the ability to change speed and dribbling height if you want to beat a defender one-on-one and drive to the basket.

The Crossover Dribble

Another method of beating your defender by dribbling is

The crossover dribble

The behind-the-back dribble

to change the direction of the dribble. This is called the *crossover dribble*. As you approach the defender you lower the dribble and bounce the ball from one hand to the other, while pivoting and pushing off your back foot in the new direction. As you turn, shield the ball with your body and your non-dribbling arm.

The Reverse Dribble

The *reverse dribble* involves spinning around almost a full 360 degrees and transferring the dribble from one hand to the other. Let's say you're dribbling with your right hand. As you approach the defender, come to a stop with your left leg forward. Smoothly pivot on the balls of both feet to the right and transfer the dribble to your left hand. As you turn fully around back toward your defender, move forward around his right side using your right arm and body to shield the ball. If you start dribbling with your left hand, reverse the procedure.

The Behind-the-back Dribble

The *behind-the-back dribble* allows you to change dribbling hands by moving the ball behind your back from one side of your body to the other. If you're dribbling with your right hand, put your right foot out front as you pull the dribble back behind you and redirect the ball to your left hand by pushing it in that direction. Reverse the procedure if you start the dribble with your left hand. The behind-the-back dribble is a risky maneuver that should only be used when there's no other way to avoid losing the ball or to beat a defender.

Ball Handling and Dribbling Drills

To get the feel of the ball and practice ball control, start out with a stationary drill. You'll probably drop the ball a lot at first but don't be discouraged. Eventually you'll gain confidence and skill.

Move the ball behind your back and around your body by passing it from one hand to the other while you're standing still. Don't forget to use your fingers only, not your palms. Do this for 30 seconds in one direction and then in the opposite direction. Next, with your feet spread shoulder-width apart use the same technique to pass the ball around your knees, 30 seconds in one direction and 30 seconds the other way. Pass the ball around each leg, then between and around both legs in a figure eight. See if you can keep it going in one continuous motion for 30 seconds.

If you don't know how to dribble at all, start the following drills standing still, gradually moving faster and faster. Spend some time on the high-speed high-bounce dribble, but concentrate on the low-bounce dribble. Don't forget to change the pace and, when you can, the direction of the dribble.

Before you start to move check out your stance. Are your knees bent, your shoulders slightly hunched, your head up? Is the arm you're not dribbling with ready to shield the ball? O.K., let's go!

This first drill is really five drills in one. It will let you practice all your dribbling techniques and also help build up your stamina. In this drill you dribble the length of the court and back five times. (If you don't have a full court available you can do the same drill on a half court by doubling back from the end line to the midcourt line.)

The first time down the court, use the high-bounce dribble, bouncing the ball between waist- and chest-high. Go as fast as you can without losing control of the ball and finish off with a layup. On the way back use the same technique but dribble and shoot with your opposite hand. Don't forget to use your fingers and *not* your palms.

The second time down the court, go into a deeper crouch and use the low-bounce control dribble. When you reach the top of the backcourt key (at the end of the foul circle closest to where you started out) pretend there's a defender waiting for you and switch dribbling hands. Switch back to avoid another "defender" at the midcourt line and again when you reach the top of the frontcourt

? **WHY DOESN'T** my coach let me play more?

It can get pretty discouraging when you don't get to play as much as you'd like to. The only solution to that problem is to practice harder and to make the most of every playing opportunity. Ask your coach what areas of your game need work, and be prepared to put in extra practice time developing those skills. And always be a good sport when you're not on the court by offering encouragement and cheers for your teammates who are playing.

key. Then pull up at the foul line and put up a set shot or jump shot. Follow your shot for a possible rebound in case you miss. Repeat your moves on the way back, remembering to throw off your "defender" by changing your pace occasionally. If you're practicing with someone else you can take turns acting as the defender, but you shouldn't attempt to steal the ball until both of you have started to master your dribbling skills.

The third time down the court, practice the reverse dribble as you approach each real or imaginary defender. Pivot on both feet and switch dribbling hands as you turn and shield the ball as you pass the defender. Finish off with a shot from the foul line, then repeat in the other direction.

On your fourth trip, use a zigzag pattern to work on the crossover dribble. Start at one corner of the court and dribble diagonally to the backcourt key. Then switch hands and continue dribbling toward the point where the sideline meets the midcourt line. When you get there, switch the ball back to the original hand and dribble toward the top of the frontcourt key. Finish off with a shot from the free throw line and repeat the drill in the opposite direction.

On your fifth trip down the floor, practice going around defenders by using the behind-the-back dribble and finish off with a layup.

Here's another good drill that uses the entire court. The idea here is to practice changing direction and changing dribbling hands. Whenever you make a left turn you should do it with a right-handed dribble, and whenever you make a right turn you should do it with a left-handed dribble.

Using the low-bounce dribble, begin in one corner and dribble along the endline to the opposite corner. Then turn, switching your dribbling hand, and dribble upcourt. When you're even with the backcourt foul line, turn and switch hands again and dribble back across court. On your way to the opposite sideline, follow the outline of the key for extra dribbling practice. When you get there, turn and dribble upcourt again.

The rest of the drill follows this same pattern. Turn and come back across court when you reach the midcourt line, when you reach the frontcourt foul line and when you reach the opposite endline. Finish off the drill by driving under the basket and shooting a reverse layup.

A terrific drill for the control dribble uses the routine you practiced in the figure-eight ball handling drill. Start out by dribbling the ball around one of your legs, switching hands as you do so. Then dribble around the other leg and wind up by dribbling figure eights. Start slowly and build up speed as you go.

The last dribbling drill is called the *dislodge drill*. It's an excellent way to practice the entire range of dribbling skills: ball control, keeping your head up, changing hands on the dribble and protecting the ball. It's also a lot of fun. You and a friend each take a ball and go into one of the foul circles or and confined area. Then as you both try to maintain your own dribble, each of you should attempt to dislodge or knock away your opponent's ball.

Passing

The greatest players of all time, from the Boston Celtics' Bob Cousy to the Los Angeles Lakers' Magic Johnson, have all been multi-talented. Almost without exception, the skill common to all great players is the ability to find the open man with a pass. Larry Bird of the Celtics has always scored points and pulled down rebounds but what makes him special is his ability and willingness to pass the ball. Along with Bird and Michael Jordan of the Chicago Bulls, Magic Johnson is considered to be one of the five or six greatest players in the history of the game. But he has never led his own team in season scoring average! Yet the leadership and passing skills he began establishing in junior high school have helped the Lakers win five NBA championships. Magic has played in the All-Star game each of his 10 seasons and was twice named the league's Most Valuable Player.

A really good pass is a thing of beauty. The passer gets the ball to a teammate at precisely the right spot and at exactly the right time. There's nothing that turns on a team (or a gym full of fans) like a basket that comes off a great "feed." A really gifted passer raises the level of everyone on his team—and good passing is often contagious.

The type of pass you use and the speed and height at which you throw it will always depend on the situation you're in. Because different situations call for different reactions, it's important you to learn seven basic passes. We'll also discuss the behind-the-back pass. It's riskier than the others because it's more difficult to complete. But when it is used appropriately and not to show off, it can be very effective.

Although the types of passes differ, these aspects of passing are always the same:

● All passing is done with the fingertips, never the palms.

● Your fingers should be spread as wide as is comfortable for you because the wider the spread, the greater the control of the ball.

● Your wrists must remain flexible. Proper wrist action is as basic to passing a basketball as it is to hitting a baseball.

● The follow-through is just as important as the wind-up or the release.

The Chest Pass

The *chest pass* is the most commonly used pass because it gets the ball to a teammate quickly. It is made from the ready position. Here's how it works: Face the teammate you're going to pass the ball to. Keep your head up and your knees slightly bent. Spread your fingers wide and hold the ball at chest level. Your hands should be slightly behind and above the center of the ball and your elbows should be slightly bent out from your sides. As you extend your arms to release the ball, take a step toward the receiver. Your wrists should snap forward and upward as you finish your follow-through.

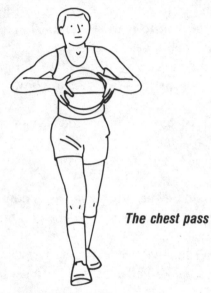 

The chest pass

The Two-handed Bounce Pass

The *two-handed bounce pass* is often used to go under the outstretched arms of a defender, and it's a controlled way to pass to a teammate who's moving for the basket. It uses the same technique as the chest pass, except that you snap your arms and wrists downward. Bounce the ball so that it reaches the receiver about waist high.

The Underhand Pass

The *underhand pass* is a soft pass that's effective only over a short distance, such as when you want to hand off to a teammate who is nearby. It can be made with either one hand or two. The two-handed version is also called the *shovel pass*. To make this pass, place your fingers on the lower half of the ball, with your palms facing each other and your thumbs on the sides of the ball. As you extend your arms to release the ball, take a step toward the receiver. Keep your wrists locked as you follow through. The ball should be delivered to the receiver waist high.

You can throw the one-handed version of the pass over a greater distance and with more speed. Try this only if you can spread your fingers wide enough to control the ball with one hand.

To make the pass, put your fingers underneath the ball. Draw the ball back alongside your body as if you were preparing to roll a bowling ball. At the same time step forward with your opposite foot, bend that knee and come up on the ball of the back foot. Then swing your arm forward in a sidearm motion and follow through in a strong upward arc.

The Two-handed Overhead Pass

The *two-handed overhead pass* is a favorite of defensive rebounders who want to make a pass to a teammate upcourt. It is used to go over the defender's arms. Because you can generate distance and speed with this pass, it's used as an outlet pass to get the ball away from a knot of players so someone can bring it down the court quickly. The overhead pass can also be used to get the ball to a player in the low post (near the basket but outside the lane).

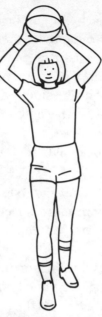

The two-handed overhead pass

Start by gripping the ball on its sides with your thumbs pointing up. With your elbows bent slightly, raise the ball above your head. As you take a step in the direction of the receiver, rotate your wrists back and down and bring the ball back behind your head. Then bring the ball forward again, extending your arms. Release the ball when your arms are almost straight. As you do so, snap your wrists down to put some power into the pass. Always remember to follow through.

If you want to deliver the pass at chest height and no higher, don't let go of the ball until your arms are fully extended in front of you. When you want to lob the ball into the low post, you should release it when it's still above your head. When you release the ball your wrists should snap up.

The Baseball Pass

The *baseball pass* is a one-handed pass that is used to throw the ball a long way. It is thrown with a motion similar to the one a baseball catcher uses to throw the ball to second base on a steal attempt. That means this pass is thrown like a line drive. It shouldn't be used to lob the ball.

Holding the ball in one hand (you may want to steady the ball with your other hand as you get the ball into position) bend the elbow of your throwing arm and bring the ball back to a position right behind your ear. Keeping the throwing hand behind the ball, step toward the receiver with your opposite foot pointing your free hand at the receiver, and throw the ball by bringing your arm forward in an overhand motion. You should throw at the same time you are stepping forward. Follow through by completely extending your arm and snapping your wrist down.

It's important to use the straight overhand motion because if you use a sidearm delivery, you'll wind up throwing a spinner that will curve and be difficult to catch. This pass will be tough to do if your hand isn't big enough yet to control the ball. If that's true, just work on the other passes.

The Hook Pass

The *hook pass* is used mainly by taller players either when they pass to a teammate cutting to the basket or when they're being tied up by smaller defenders. To throw the pass, hold the ball on its bottom with your fingertips. Don't let it sit in the palm of your hand. Extend your passing arm behind you and extend your non-shooting arm toward the receiver. Then with your arm straight and your elbow locked, bring your passing arm up in an arc over your shoulder. Release the ball just as your hand passes your head and snap your wrist forward and down.

The hook pass

The Off-the-dribble Pass

The *off-the-dribble pass* is made while you are dribbling. This makes it very effective because the quick delivery often catches the defense napping. To make the pass, bring your dribbling hand down, but instead of tapping the ball on the top, put your fingertips in back of it. With your elbow bent, push the ball forward with a sharp flick of the wrist. You can deliver the pass either on a line through the air or on a bounce.

Master passer Earvin "Magic" Johnson of the Los Angeles Lakers handing out a perfect off-the-dribble pass. By leaning into the man guarding him, Magic creates extra space for the person who will receive the pass!

The behind-the-back pass

The Behind-the-back Pass

The *behind-the-back pass* is a very tricky pass and is just as likely to fool your teammates as your opponents. If you're going to pass with your right hand, step forward with your left foot. Grab the front of the ball and swing your arm around your back. Let the ball go when you have extended your arm as fully as possible, using your wrist to guide the ball. But keep in mind that in most situations you will probably make the play more efficiently if you use one of the basic passes described above.

Receiving the Ball

Before you can dribble, pass or shoot, you're going to have to get the ball in your hands. And that means you'll have to get away from your defender and know how to catch the ball.

If you want a teammate to pass the ball to you, you must find a way to get open. Sometimes that involves moving away from the player with the ball and other times it means moving toward that player. Whatever direction you move in, you'll improve your chances of getting free if you first fake going in another direction. You can do that by dipping your head and shoulder one way and then quickly moving the opposite way. You can also fake out your opponent by taking a step in one direction and then sprinting in the opposite direction.

Once you're in the clear and the ball is on the way, you have to catch it. To catch a pass, spread your fingers as wide as you comfortably can. Your hands should be cupped, palms out, and held so closely together that they're

The correct way to receive a pass and move into position for a jump shot

almost touching. Your body should be in the ready position with your feet spread shoulder-width apart, one foot a little ahead of the other in the direction the pass is coming from. Your knees should be slightly bent and you should be leaning in the direction of the pass with your arms bent at the elbows, extended to receive the ball.

Be aware of what's going on around you before you receive a pass in order to know whether you should shoot, pass or dribble after you catch the ball. Once the ball is in the air, always watch it right into your hands.

To catch a pass that is thrown below your waist, deepen your crouch by bending your knees and point your fingers down with your pinkies almost touching. To catch a ball above your waist, point your fingers up with your thumbs almost touching. Use your fingers and upper palms to grasp the ball and immediately bring it in to your body. If you have to jump for a pass or make a running catch, make sure you don't take any extra steps. Come to a complete and sudden stop; if you don't, you'll be called for walking.

When you're catching a pass, always move toward the ball. If you wait for it to come to you, a defender will have more time to try and intercept it, swat it away, or get into better position to cover you once you get the ball.

Passing and Receiving Drills

Use these drills to sharpen your passing skills and to practice the entire range of passes. Remember to follow through and to "lead" a teammate who is on the move, which means throwing the ball to where you *expect* your

This University of Maryland player is straddling the three-point line, looking to pass the ball inside. Maryland lost the 1989 woman's NCAA tournament semifinal game to Tennessee University, 77–65; Tennessee went on to win the title.

teammate to be. When you don't have anyone to practice with, see if you can put a target up on a wall or a fence. (But make sure you have permission and that you're not going to break anything!)

When you're practicing with someone else be sure to concentrate on your receiving as well as your passing. Every passing drill should also be a receiving drill. Stand about 10 to 12 feet away from your partner and practice all the basic passes. Make sure you're using your fingers and following through correctly. If your hands are small and you have trouble controlling the ball when you're delivering the chest and bounce passes, put your hands behind the ball more, with your thumbs almost touching. If you have a third player to practice with you can add a defender to the drill, with each of you taking turns.

After you're comfortable performing the passes standing still, start passing while you move down the court, still about 10 to 12 feet apart. Begin at a walk and gradually build up speed. Be sure to throw the pass ahead of your partner so that he doesn't have to slow down to receive the ball.

When you can do the chest pass and the bounce pass perfectly at full speed, try to do the chest pass without letting the ball touch the floor. As you run straight ahead, parallel to a teammate, pass the ball back and forth, turning only your torso to make and receive the passes. Remember not to walk—that is, take too many steps—between passes. In a real game you can't advance the ball more than one step without dribbling, and you want to simulate game conditions whenever possible!

You can practice the overhead pass, the hook pass and

the baseball pass by standing in front of one basket a
throwing each of the passes to a partner running towarc
midcourt. Practice each pass five times from the right side
and five times from the left side.

Chapter 6

PUTTING IT ALL TOGETHER

In the earlier chapters we have broken the game of basketball down into parts. Now let's look at the way the individual player functions within a team.

Offensive Tactics

There's an old saying in basketball: "What you give up, you'll get back." That's a perfect description of the most fundamental of all basketball plays, the *give-and-go*. In the give-and-go, the player with the ball passes to a teammate and then immediately cuts away, breaks for the basket and quickly receives a return pass. The reason this play works so often is that a defensive player tends to relax slightly after the person he is guarding passes the ball. You can fool your defender if, after you pass the ball, you give a head, shoulder or foot fake away from the direction in which you're going to cut. Besides being a very effective play, the give-and-go is useful because it promotes good teamwork.

Another version of the give-and-go is called the *pinch post*. You pass the ball to a player in the high post and then cut so closely around that teammate that the player guarding you gets left behind, leaving you free to receive a return pass and leaving an open lane to an easy basket. In the pinch post play your teammate has set up what is called a *screen* or *pick*. The purpose of setting screens is to keep a defender from covering the man with the ball. This is done by getting in the defender's path and blocking his way, which frees the man on offense.

To set a pick for a teammate you should position yourself in the path of the man guarding him. This may sound

Setting a screen or pick.
Player number 7
is about to "pick off"
the person guarding the player with the ball.

like you're setting yourself up for a potentially violent collision. You are. That's why several rules have been established governing the use of picks; breaking them results in a turnover or a foul shot, depending on the violation.

● Once you've gotten into position you cannot move while the player with the ball is near you.

● You cannot use your hands, arms, legs or feet to keep a defender from "fighting" his way through the pick you have set, even though you might be getting jostled or pushed around.

● If you want to set a pick for a player who is dribbling the ball, you must get into position at least one full step before the defender gets to the spot you've selected for the pick. If you want to set a pick for a player who has the

...ll and is about to start dribbling, you must get into posi-...ion before the player starts to dribble.

Setting screens is a good way to get players open for outside shots and it also can set up another exciting play known as the *pick-and-roll*. Suppose you set a pick for a teammate who is dribbling toward you. You pick off your teammate's defender but the person guarding you jumps out to guard your teammate. At that instant you should pivot away from the defender and *roll* toward the basket while keeping your eye on the ball. (The word "roll" is used because your move toward the basket is most likely to be a spinning, or rolling, motion.) If your teammate is alert, you should receive a pass for an easy two-pointer.

Another effective maneuver for you and your team-mates to try is the *backdoor* play. It's a variation of the give-and-go, involving three players rather than two. The third player who shoots has not done any passing. The play begins when a player passes the ball to a teammate in the high or low post. If the player guarding you directs his attention to the player in the post, you should immediately cut for the basket, looking to your teammate with the ball while you run. She'll get the pass to you and with the defenders caught off guard expecting a shot by your teammate, you'll go in for the basket "through the back door."

A *fast break* is a situation rather than one play. It is when the offense moves the ball from one end of the court to the other so quickly that the defense is at a disadvantage because its players are caught out of position. The offense's advantage can involve one player ahead of the field, or a two-on-one situation (two players against one

Fast break, part one: James Worthy of the Los Angeles Lakers is about to pick up a loose ball and race downcourt. Meanwhile, Isiah Thomas and one of his teammates on the Detroit Pistons struggle to get up and back on defense.

Fast break, part two: These players from Kuwait have their opponents on the run and out of position. If this cross-

court pass is successful—and it looks good so far—it could lead to an easy layup.

efender), or a three-on-two situation (three players against two defenders) or similar advantages. A fast break usually results in an easy basket. But fast breaks do more than give a team quick buckets—they can change the entire momentum of a game. You and your teammates should constantly be looking for opportunities to break out and beat your opponents down the court.

Most fast breaks start as the result of a turnover, a steal or a defensive rebound, so you have to be alert and ready to switch instantly from a defensive role to an offensive one. When you're on a fast break with a teammate or two, don't run close together; this can make it easy for the out-manned defense to make up for its disadvantage by covering two of you at once. Rather, you should each run straight downcourt, which is also known as *staying in your lane*. And always keep running toward the basket even if you're the last one down the court on the play, so you can be in position to grab a rebound and put in a follow-up shot.

Defensive Tactics

Every player on a basketball team has a defensive role as well as an offensive one. Since the goal of the offense is to score as many points as possible, the main idea on defense is to stop the other team from scoring. Blocking shots and stealing the ball are exciting plays that can turn a game around. But going for blocks and steals and missing or fouling instead can turn the game in the other direction. In most cases you're better off using sound defensive techniques. You want to limit your opponents' scoring by

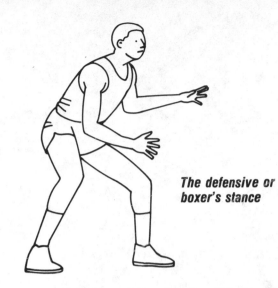

The defensive or boxer's stance

playing an aggressive style of defense that will cause them to try difficult shots and to operate from areas of the floor where they're not comfortable.

The *defensive stance* is also known as the *boxer's stance* and it's the defensive equivalent of the ready stance on offense. It puts you in position to defend against the three offensive options—the shot, the pass and the dribble. To get into the stance, you spread your feet slightly more than shoulder-width apart with one foot a little more forward than the other. Balance on the balls of your feet. Flex your knees and bend forward a little. If your left foot is in front, hold your left arm out to your side and about head high. Your right arm should be out to the side somewhere between waist- and knee-height. Both elbows should be slightly bent and your hands should be open with the fingers spread. Your back should be straight, your head up and your eyes focused on the mid-section of the player you're guarding. When that person

Defending against the shot

has the ball, position yourself approximately an arm's length away from her.

To keep your opponent from getting to open floor space, *overplay* her by a half step in the direction of the open space. This means that instead of taking up your defensive stance positioned exactly in front of her, you'll actually be "cheating" a bit to one side. For example if you're guarding a player who is to the right of the foul circle (her right, your left), you would overplay your opponent a half step toward the middle of the court. This keeps her to the outside, denying her a direct drive to the basket.

To move quickly when you're in the defensive stance use a sliding or shuffle step. If you want to go left, begin with the right foot and take a short shuffle-step to the left. Then take a short sliding step with the left foot. Keep on moving this way as long as your opponent continues in that direction. To move to the right, reverse the procedure. To move backward, take a short step back with your front foot. Shuffle back with your other foot and follow your opponent. Reverse the procedure for moving forward. Never use a crossover step. A crossover step is when you move sideways by moving one foot over and across the other. It's useful for baseball outfielders but you'll tie yourself up in knots if you try to use it on a basketball court.

When you're guarding a player who doesn't have the ball, position yourself so you can be close to your opponent and still see the ball. One elbow should point toward your opponent and the other toward the ball. If your opponent is far from the ball and far outside her scoring range, guard her loosely. There's no point in pressing a player

Defending against the dribble

*Even the Chicago Bulls Michael Jordan has to play defense!
Here the NBA's most feared scoring machine sets up in the*

basic defensive stance, with his arms at his sides, as one
of the Washington Bullets calls for the ball.

who isn't in a threatening position. But stay alert and remember that any time your opponent or the ball moves, you should move, too.

Defending the post requires a special note because the player in the post position almost always plays with her back to the basket. When you're defending against a player in the low post who doesn't have the ball, you should *front* the player. Fronting means that you position yourself between your opponent and the ball. You always have to watch out, though, for lob passes over your head. If you're guarding a player in the high post who doesn't have the ball you should play behind that person while overplaying in the direction of the ball. As the offense passes the ball and as the post player moves, constantly shift your position. When the post player receives the ball, try to prevent her from making a driving move to the basket. And when the player takes a shot, don't forget to keep your body between her and the basket.

Types of Defenses

There are three basic defenses in basketball: *man-to-man* (sometimes called *person-to-person* in girls' and women's leagues), *zone* and some *combination* of zone and man-to-man. Each has variations and can be used with varying degrees of defensive pressure. If you're playing against a team that shoots poorly from the outside, your coach will most likely have your team play a *sagging* defense. That means your team will guard the outside players loosely while concentrating on limiting inside scoring opportunities. When you do that you also create good rebounding positions for yourself. If on the other hand the other team

110

Patrick Ewing of the New York Knicks calls for the ball inside. Defending Ewing in the low post is no picnic. Front him and he'll move right by you for the dunk; play him like this and he has lots of room to maneuver.

? WHY ME? (Or, how I lost the game for my team)

It can seem pretty bleak when you miss a shot at the buzzer that could have won the game but don't blame yourself for the loss. Basketball is a team sport. Individuals don't win or lose games—teams do. If you play in enough games you're going to hit some big buckets and you're going to miss some, too. No one wins or loses all the time. Even the greatest players sometimes miss in clutch situations. In 1989 Michael Jordan missed a foul shot in the last seconds of a playoff game against Cleveland that allowed the Cavaliers to come back and win the game. "I was crushed after I missed that free throw," he said. But Michael bounced right back and led his team to victory in the next game. Hang in there and you will bounce back too.

has excellent outside shooters, your coach will have you playing very close to them, concentrating on all of them equally. No matter which defensive alignment your coach calls for, you always assume the basic defensive stance.

In a man-to-man defensive alignment, your main job is to guard a single player. But you also need to keep your eye on the ball and be ready to give defensive support to a teammate. In one-on-one defense keep yourself between the player and the basket she's shooting at, unless you're guarding a player in the low post. You want to prevent the player you're guarding from getting the ball. And when the player you're guarding *has* the ball within scoring range, first try to stop the drive—a layup is more likely to score than an outside shot.

There are many different types of zone defenses. Two of the most common are a 1–3–1 and a 2–3. In a 1–3–1, one player is stationed up high around the top of the foul circle, three players are strung out in a row right below the foul line and one player is down deep near the basket. In a 2–3, two players are up high and three players down low. Regardless of the type of zone defense being played, your first responsibility is the ball. Your secondary responsibility is an area of the court rather than a specific player. Any player who enters your area or zone is your responsibility for as long as she remains there. You don't stand in just one spot when you play a zone. Because you have an area to defend, you have to keep shifting around depending on where the ball goes.

Combination defenses are used when a coach wants to play a zone defense and at the same time give special attention to one or two offensive threats on the opposing team. The coach might use a combination defense such as a *box-and-one*. In the box-and-one, four players form a square-shaped zone defense while the fifth player guards the opposing team's star scorer one-on-one.

An important factor in playing effective defense is *anticipation*--the ability to figure out what your opponent is going to do next. Anticipation isn't like ESP or guess-work. It's based on finding out what your opponent can do and likes to do and then using the information to figure out what your opponent *will* do. For example, if the player you're guarding can only dribble with the right hand, then you can just about eliminate the possibility that that player will drive to her left. Instead, you anticipate a move to the right and adjust your position to stop her.

*Anticipation in action! Charles Barkley of the Philadelphia
76ers stopping what his opponent thought would be an easy
shot by getting to the spot first and going up strong.*

Naturally, it's usually not that simple. There are playe who can drive to either side, shoot layups with either hand and shoot from the outside. In that case you have to know which side they're most comfortable operating from and look for clues that will tell whether they're going to shoot or drive and to which side. The only way to pick up those clues is through experience and careful study of your opponent. Once you've gathered information about your opposing team you'll usually be able to make the right move.

Being skillful at anticipation will also help alert you to developing situations. For example, if you see that someone is about to set a screen so that the person you're guarding can move past you, you can beat the defender to the spot and avoid being "picked off." If you're late and the person is able to set the screen you can try to fight through it or you can tell a teammate to help out by calling "switch." Don't forget, though, that as soon as you call the switch and your teammate picks up the player you were guarding, you have to guard the player your teammate had been guarding. Otherwise, your opponent ends up free to maneuver.

This kind of communication is absolutely necessary for playing good team defense. Teammates must learn to help each other by calling out switches and picks and pointing out other potential problems and opportunities. For instance, if you see that an opponent has been left unguarded, shout "man open" and make sure someone— you, if necessary-—goes over to cover. Or you could shout "box out" as a reminder to your teammates when a rebound is about to come down. Even a general comment ch as, "Let's play good 'D' here!" can help keep your team fired up. So don't be shy!

The most important thing to remember is that defense, like rebounding, depends more on concentration and dedication than technique and strategy. You have to *want* to play defense to play it well.

GLOSSARY

Air ball: a shot that misses the basket completely, not touching the rim or backboard, and was not blocked or tipped

Assist: a pass to a teammate that leads directly to a basket

Backcourt: the half of the court on which a team is playing defense; also, the two guards' positions combined are sometimes called a team's backcourt

Basket: the metal hoop through which points are scored; also, the score itself, as in, "We need a basket!"

Blocking: a foul committed by a defensive player when he moves into the legal path of an offensive player and causes contact, or by an offensive player without the ball who moves into the legal path of a defensive player and causes contact

Boxing out: keeping your body between the basket and your opponent when going for a rebound

Charging: a foul committed by an offensive player who has the ball and who runs into a defensive player who is standing still

Court sense: being aware of what is happening on the court, including player position and game situation

Cut: a quick move by an offensive player, usually toward the basket

Double dribble: a violation that occurs when a player stops dribbling, then starts again

Double-teaming: when two defensive players guard one offensive player

Dribble: to move the ball by bouncing it; the only legal way for an individual player to move with the ball while maintaining possession

Drive: an offensive player's move toward the basket; also, the act of *driving*, as in, "Smith is driving in for a layup!"

End lines: the lines forming the short ends of the basketball court

Fast break: a play in which the offensive team moves quickly toward the basket at which it is shooting, catching the defense off guard and outnumbered in the frontcourt

Field goal: *see* Field shot

Field shot: a shot taken from anywhere on the court; field shots or *field goals* count as either two or three points, depending on where the shooter is in relation to the three-point line

Follow-through: the completion of a shooting or passing motion after the player has released the ball

Foul: *see* Personal foul

Foul circle: the circle at the outer end of the free-throw line

Foul shot: an unchallenged shot taken from the foul line by the player who was fouled; also called a *free throw*

Free throw: *see* Foul shot

Frontcourt: the half of the court on which a team is playing offense; also, the center and forward positions combined are sometimes called a team's frontcourt

Give-and-go: to pass to a teammate, then get a short pass back from him as you cut for the basket

Goaltending: touching a ball while it is in the imaginary cylinder above the rim or is on its downward flight toward the basket; it is illegal for both the offensive and defensive players

High post: the offensive area just outside the free-throw circle

Hoop: the rim of the basket

Jump ball: when the referee puts the ball into play by tossing it into the air between two opposing players

Jump shot: a field goal attempt taken with one hand while the player is airborne

Key: the free-throw lane, including the foul circle

Lane: *see* Key

Layup: a one-hand shot made from close to the basket

Low post: the offensive area outside the key but close to the basket

Man-to-man defense: a style of defense in which each player on a team is responsible for guarding a specific opponent

Midcourt line: the line that divides the court in half; also called the *10-second line* because the offensive team has 10 seconds from the time the ball is put into play in its defensive zone to dribble or pass the ball across the midcourt line

Offensive foul: a foul committed by a player when his team has possession of the ball

Palming the ball: a violation of the dribbling rules in which the palm of the hand is used to turn the ball over by scooping it up and then down in one motion

Personal foul: when there is illegal body contact between opposing players

Person-to-person defense: *see* man-to-man defense

Pick: when an offensive player acts as a shield between a teammate and the player guarding the teammate so the teammate can attempt a field goal or drive around the defender; also called a *screen*

Pivot: a method of turning on one foot; another name for the center or post position

Press: a style of defense in which the defensive team tightly guards the offensive team; the two most common are the *full-court press*, in which the offensive players are guarded tightly wherever they are, and the *half-court press*, in which the defense doesn't apply pressure until the offensive players have moved the ball across the midcourt line

Rebound: a shot that bounces off the rim or backboard; also, gaining possession of the ball by catching a missed shot by a player

Screen: *see* Pick

Steps: *see* Traveling

Switch: a technique in defensive play in which a teammate leaves the player he is guarding and switches to the player that a teammate has been guarding; a switch usually occurs when the offense sets a pick against a defender

Technical foul: a violation of the game's rules of conduct or procedure; a technical foul results in the awarding of a free throw and possession of the ball to the non-offending team

Ten-second rule: the offensive team has 10 seconds from the time the ball is put into play in its defensive zone to dribble or pass the ball across the midcourt line

Three-point play: a play in which a shooter is fouled in the act of scoring a field goal and then sinks the foul shot

Three-point shot: a field goal attempt made from beyond a certain distance; that distance varies from league to league

Three-second rule: an offensive player may not stay in the lane for more than three seconds; violation of the rule results in a turnover

Traveling: taking more than one step without a dribble while in possession of the ball; violation of the rule results in a turnover; also called *steps* and *walking*

Turnover: loss of possession of the ball because of a misplay or an infraction of the rules

Violation: an infraction of the rules not classified as a foul, examples include *three-seconds* and *traveling*

Walking: *see* Traveling

Zone defense: any of a wide variety of defenses in which the primary responsibility of the defender is an area of the court rather than a particular player

Interior design by Bernard Springsteel
Illustrations by Stanford Kay-Paragraphics

Photography Credits

Mark Lennihan/AP Wide World: 6
David Madison: 9, 25
UPI/Bettmann Newsphotos: 12
Mitchell Layton/Duomo: 19, 108
Kenneth Garrett/FPG Int'l: 31
Rick Rickman/Duomo: 35
Jerry Wachter/Sports Illustrated: 37, 114
Diane Johnson: 38
John Turner/FPG Int'l: 49
Richard Mackson/FPG Int'l: 53, 73
Noren Trotman: 58, 62, 111
Brian Drake: 70
Peter Read Miller/Sports Illustrated: 89, 93
Bob Thomas Sports Photography: 103
John McDonough/Sports Illustrated: 15, 101
Mike Valeri/FPG Int'l: 97

About the Author

Richard Brenner is the author of many sports books for young adults, among them The World Series: The Great Contests, The Complete Super Bowl Story Games I–XXIV, Pro Football's All-Time All-Star Team, *and three dual biographies:* Michael Jordan/Magic Johnson, John Elway/Bernie Kosar *and* Roger Clemens/Darryl Strawberry. *He lives in Syosset, New York, with his wife, Anita and children, Hallie and Jason.*